P9-BYT-567

Presented to

_____

By _____

In Loving Remembrance of

_____

On This Day

_____

Will I
See
My Pet
in Heaven?

CHILDREN'S EDITION

Friar Jack Wintz

PARACLETE PRESS
BREWSTER, MASSACHUSETTS

Will I See My Pet in Heaven?

2011 First Printing

Copyright © 2011 by Jack Wintz

ISBN: 978-1-61261-098-6

Library of Congress Cataloging-in-Publication Data
Wintz, Jack.
  Will I see my pet in heaven? / Jack Wintz. – Children's ed.
    p. cm.
  Rev. ed. of: I will see you in heaven.
  ISBN 978-1-61261-098-6 (hard cover)
  1. Animals–Religious aspects–Christianity–Juvenile literature. 2. Future life–Christianity–Juvenile literature. I. Wintz, Jack. I will see you in heaven. II. Title.
  BT746.W562 2011
  231.7–dc23   2011047139

10 9 8 7 6 5 4 3 2 1

Published by Paraclete Press
Brewster, Massachusetts
www.paracletepress.com

Will I See My Pet in Heaven? is also designed to help children who have recently lost a pet. You may want to add the words "In Loving Memory" followed by the name of the child's beloved pet on the opening Presentation Page.

Manufactured by Thomson-Shore, Dexter, MI (USA); RMA578LS921, December, 2011

A Small Question with a Big Answer

Let me tell you a story.

This story is about my young friend Eva Maria, who stopped to see me one afternoon at my office in Cincinnati. She had a question she wanted to ask.

"Today at school, one of the kids told me that only humans go to heaven," she said. "I almost started to cry. Is that true, Friar Jack?"

She went on: " . . . because my dog Daisy is my best friend. When I get home she jumps into my arms and licks my face. *Wouldn't* God want her to be with me in heaven?"

Then, Eva Maria looked at me, waiting for the answer she hoped for.

"God loves you and Daisy more than you even know, Eva Maria," I said. "If we trust in God's love and goodness, then we believe that God wants each of us to be happy, both here on earth and for eternity in heaven. Honestly, what kind of heaven would it be if the animals we love so much can't be with us?" I asked.

My young friend nodded. "If only people were in heaven, it would be boring." Then, she smiled.

I laughed and agreed with her. "Whatever it takes to make you happy in heaven, God will make sure that it's there. We know God cares for all of us and wants what is best for all creatures."

"Then I know I'll see Daisy again!" Eva Maria said.

We don't know everything God has planned for us in heaven. But there are many good reasons for you to believe that your dog, cat, fish, hamster, snake, ferret, iguana—or any other creature that God created—will go to heaven when it dies. God has given us clues and hints in stories from the Bible and in the teachings of my favorite saint, Francis of Assisi.

I said all of that to Eva Maria that day when she asked me her question.

"I remember that St. Francis loved the animals and the birds," called out Eva Maria as she skipped away. "He called them his brothers and sisters. But I don't have time to hear more stories right now. My mom is waiting outside for me!" Much happier than when she had walked in, my young friend was already out the door.

"I'll come back another day!" she called back to me.

Most of us have the same question as Eva Maria, whether we're children or grownups. "Will I see my pet in heaven?"

We have a deep desire to know if we will see our pets again, and all the other lovely creatures who live with us on the earth that God made.

What will become of them after they die?

Have You Heard of Saint Francis of Assisi?

I have been a Franciscan friar for over fifty years, and over that very long time I've thought about this question a lot. I love the stories of St. Francis of Assisi and his close friendship with animals, and these stories have shaped the way that I view these things. Perhaps you've also heard the stories of this brown-robed friar preaching to the birds, releasing Brother Rabbit from a trap, or letting Sister Raven serve as his "alarm clock" to awaken him for early morning prayer.

You haven't? Well, then, you will!

You might even know that St. Francis wrote a wonderful poem, or song, called *The Canticle of the Creatures,* or sometimes *The Canticle of Brother Sun.* In this song, Francis invites all his brother and sister creatures to praise their Creator—Brother Sun and Sister Moon, Brother Fire and Sister Water, as well as Sister Earth, our mother, with all her sweet fruits and brightly colored flowers.

I'll tell you about some of these things in this book.

What the Bible Says

The Bible says, "In the beginning, God created heaven and earth." Right? In other words, our God, who is caring toward all, created one big family. And if that is true, doesn't it make sense that God's saving care would include not only human beings, but the whole family of creation?

I believe that's what St. Francis saw when he read the Bible. He understood that our whole world was connected, not only physically here on this earth but through God's love for us, and even after we die.

When you learn about the ecology of Planet Earth in school—for example, about how the environment in one place is affected by a change happening in another place—you might think about Francis, who was named the patron saint of ecology. He brought the word of God to all of God's creation, talking to the rabbits and the robins just as he talked to the people in the villages he walked through.

The question we ask after a beloved pet dies—"Will I see my pet in heaven?"—may seem small on the surface, but the answer is a big one for the whole created world. What would it mean if all creatures were one family? How would it change our understanding about God, and about how we relate to God and to each other?

And It Was Very Good

Now, grab a Bible, if you have one, and look at the first chapter of Genesis. That's the very first chapter of the Bible!

In the earliest verses you will read about how darkness covered everything until God created light to separate the darkness from the light. Then it says, "And God saw that the light was good."

Soon we read that God separated the earth from the seas. Again, the Bible says, "And God saw that it was good."

Then God added plants, trees, and fruit. What comes after that? "And God saw that it was good."

On the fourth day, God put two great lights in the sky, the greater light to rule the day and the lesser light to rule the night. We call those lights the sun and the moon. In Genesis chapter one it then says once again, "And God saw that it was good."

St. Francis would call these two great lights Brother Sun and Sister Moon.

On the fifth day, God created sea monsters and birds of all kinds. "And God saw that it was good."

On the sixth day, God made land creatures of every kind—"cattle and creeping things and wild animals of the earth of every kind. And God saw that it was good."

Also on the sixth day, God made human beings, saying, "Let us make humankind in our image, according to our likeness; and let them have dominion over the fish of the sea, and over the birds of the air, and over cattle, and over all the wild animals of the earth."

Finally, in Genesis 1:31, "God saw everything that he had made, and indeed, it was very good."

This label of "*very* good," which God places upon both human and nonhuman creatures, seems to show God's desire to have both kinds of creatures share in the original Garden of Paradise, where peace and harmony reigned between God and human beings, and among all creatures. I believe that this is the first place where the Bible tells us that God loves and cares forever about everything that he created. Certainly, God is not going to create and then *ignore* what he sees as "very good" creatures!

God does *everything* out of love, and this includes the creation of our world. Our God is a God of overflowing love, goodness, and beauty who is ready to give over everything to those he loves. This goodness is reflected in the whole family of creation.

It makes sense to me that the same loving Creator who arranged for these animals and other nonhuman creatures to enjoy happiness in the original Garden of Eden would not want to leave them out of the *final* paradise in heaven. If they were happy and enjoying God's presence, according to their abilities, in that first Garden, God would want them to be happy and enjoy the same in heaven.

All the creatures God has ever made were created as good, all of creation was very good together, and there's no reason why that should change in the eternal future. What will it exactly be like in heaven? I don't know. No one knows for sure. But I *do* know that in Scripture St. Paul tells us simply to trust in "all that God has prepared for those who love him" (1 Cor. 2:9 JB).

Blessing the Animals

When I try to imagine heaven, where animals and humans live together in peace and harmony, I often think of the animal blessings that I have taken part in. On October fourth, the Feast Day of St. Francis, churches all over the world hold "Blessing of the Animals" services, in which creatures are offered special blessings in church as members of God's family. Children and grownups bring their pets to a park or a church courtyard with lots of trees and flowers in it, and perhaps a fountain or pool of water.

Sometimes, when people bring their pets from different parts of town, there can be a little trouble getting along. Dogs start barking at cats and people struggle to keep their animals from fighting, growling, and hissing. But often in my experience, once the blessings begin, a spirit of harmony and peace settles over everyone, pets and people. It can even remind us of the Garden of Eden!

When we consider the story of Adam and Eve before their disobedience, and we look at the animals, the birds, the fish, the trees and plants in the Garden, they all seem to live in happy harmony with Adam and Eve.

True, the nonhuman creatures do not have human souls, and they have not been baptized into new life with God, but they have some way of being connected in order to do the things they do. An animal that shows affection and loyalty, for example, surely has some kind of "soul" or inner light that allows it to enjoy life and give great joy to its caretakers. A bird that sings a beautiful melody reflects the beauty of its Maker and gives us a bit of heaven as we listen. There are a lot of things we just don't know about eternal life with God, and one of these things is how nonhumans are part of that life.

One thing that we *do* know from the stories in Genesis is that animals, plants, and other creatures found happiness in the first Paradise. Why then would God—or anyone else—want to keep them out of the paradise that is yet to come? Just as we find clues in the book of Genesis that God wants animals and other nonhuman creatures to share such joys, so we will also find clues in other books of Scripture and in other stories.

St. Francis was not the only Servant of God who believed in the sacredness of the animal kingdom. Many years ago Blessed Mother Teresa of Calcutta sent a letter to a friend of mine who organizes a "Blessing of the Animals" each year. In it she wrote that animals, too, "are created by the same hand of God which created us. As we humans are gifted with intelligence, which the animals lack, it is our duty to protect them and to promote their well-being. We also owe it to them as they serve us with such . . . loyalty." Mother Teresa lives in heaven now, and I believe that the people and animals she loved are with her there.

Noah, the Ark, and the Dove

I'll make a guess—and I'm pretty sure I'm right—that you learned the story of Noah and the ark when you were a very young child. But here we are looking at that story for another hint that God is all in favor of your pet being with you in heaven.

The ark that Noah built is a wonderful clue to God's desire to save the whole family of creation. God's plan is not to save humankind apart from other creatures. We are all in the same boat!

Because most of the people of Noah's time were behaving badly—cheating and stealing and even killing one another—God told Noah that he was going to destroy everything living on the earth as well as the earth itself. God knew that Noah and his wife and family were the only good people, so God told Noah to build a huge ark, a boat with a roof, three decks, and a door on the side.

God showed his love and care in telling Noah to bring aboard the ark "every kind" of creature (making sure that none would go extinct) and one male and one female (so baby animals would be born, and new eggs would hatch, and so on). God didn't want Noah to pack them in the back of a big truck and rush them off to some safe place. God wanted Noah to be more caring about the details as well as about all these brother and sister creatures.

Then came the storm, when it rained for forty days and forty nights. A great flood swept away every living creature from the face of the earth. Only Noah and his family—and the animals and other creatures—were safe and sound in the ark.

After the rain stopped, Noah opened the window and sent out a dove to see if she could find dry land. On the second try, the dove came back with an olive branch, which meant the water was going down. The third time the dove flew out, she did not return, because the flood was over. All who were aboard the ark were safe. Noah and his household and all the creatures left the ark and began their lives again on the earth. The little dove who flew over the water was part of God's plan to save both the humans and the other creatures: we are actually meant to help one another reach our common salvation.

Then God made a promise—a covenant—to never again destroy human beings and other living creatures. The covenant is not simply between God and humans, but also "with every living creature that is with you, the birds, the domestic animals, and every animal of the earth with you, as many as came out of the ark," said God (Gen. 9:10). God put a rainbow in the sky and told Noah: "This is the sign of the covenant I have established between me and you and every living creature that is with you, for all future generations" (Gen. 9:12).

Thus in the story of Noah and the ark, we see that God's plan is to save the human family along with the rest of the living creatures. And God backs up this promise with the rainbow, a sign of hope, arching across the whole family of creation.

All Creatures Sing Praise to God

In the Bible's book of Psalms we find prayers in which human beings invite other creatures to praise God along with them.

One of my favorites is Psalm 148, a song-story that shows us in a beautiful way that all creatures have an important place in God's plan.

> "Praise the LORD from the heavens;
> Praise him in the heights.
> Praise him all you his angels . . .
> Praise him, sun and moon;
> Praise him, all you shining stars.
>
> Praise the LORD from the earth,
> you sea monsters and all depths;
> Fire and hail, snow and mist,
> storm winds that fulfill your word;
> You mountains and all you hills,
> you fruit trees and all you cedars;
> You wild beasts and all tame animals,
> You creeping things and you winged fowl.

> Let the kings of the earth and all peoples . . .
> Young men too, and maidens,
> Old men and boys,
> Praise the name of the LORD."

Just as in the story of the ark and the great flood, in which Noah and his family along with the larger family of nonhuman creatures are saved together, so it is in the words of this hymn. All creatures are praising God together again. We are all seeking a share in God's mercy and love, and someday, final happiness in paradise.

The Song of St. Francis

Pictures or statues of St. Francis of Assisi usually show him with his bird and animal friends and dressed in the brown robes that all the friars in his order wear (including me). But when he was young he was wealthy and dressed in fancy clothes. He loved to have fun with his friends, and he even dreamed of being a knight and winning glorious battles. As a young man, Francis went off to war—he thought that it would be a great adventure—but he was captured and then spent a year in prison. He was safe there, but he did a lot of hard thinking about his life.

Back in Assisi, Francis gave his life to God and soon found himself living among the poor and sick outcasts and humbly caring for them. He showed so much joy in his work that others asked to join Francis in his ministry to the poor. They formed into a brotherhood, and in 1209 (more than 800 years ago) the Franciscan way of life became an official religious order.

However, this early information doesn't tell us about another very important piece of Francis's life—his great love of the wonders of nature and the living creatures God placed on earth to keep us company on our journey to God. This brings us to St. Francis's great *Canticle of the Creatures.* This hymn, or song of praise to our Creator, is very much like the spirit of Psalm 148 from the Bible that we read earlier.

Francis invites us to form one family with all creatures and to sing out together in praise to our common Creator. Here are some of the words to St. Francis's famous song:

Most high, all-powerful, all-good Lord!
All praise is yours, all glory, all honor, and all blessing....
All praise be yours, my Lord,
    Through all that you have made,
And first my lord Brother Sun,
        who brings the day;
        and light you give us through him.
        How beautiful is he,
        how radiant in all his splendor!
        Of you, Most High, he bears the likeness.

All praise be yours, my Lord,

> through Sister Moon and Stars,
>
> in the heavens you have made them, bright
>
> and precious and fair.

All praise be yours, my Lord,

> through Brothers Wind and Air,
>
> and fair and stormy, all the weather's moods,
>
> by which you cherish all that you have made.

All praise be yours, my Lord,

> through Sister Water,
>
> so useful, lowly, precious, and pure.

All praise be yours, my Lord,

> through Brother Fire,
>
> through whom you brighten up the night.
>
> How beautiful is he, how merry!
>
> full of power and strength.

All praise be yours, my Lord,

> through Sister Earth, our mother,
>
> who feeds us in her sovereignty and produces
>
> various fruits and colored flowers and herbs....

Praise and bless my Lord, and give him thanks,

> And serve him with great humility.

St. Francis and the Creatures

Just as we find a spirit of great care and reverence for the creatures in St. Francis's *Canticle*, so we find in Francis's daily life the same love for every creature he met along his way.

Francis's care even included the earthworms he saw on the roadway. He would carefully pick them up and place them on the side of the road where they would be out of harm's way. Have you ever done that?

Francis saw the goodness and beauty of God in the sunset and in a clear blue lake. He was in awe of the butterfly as well as the cricket.

There are many popular stories about St. Francis and other creatures.

One day a rabbit was brought to him by a brother who had found it caught in a trap. Francis warned the rabbit to be more careful in the future. Releasing the rabbit from the trap, Francis set it on the ground and told it to go on its way. But the rabbit just hopped back to Francis and sat on his lap, wanting to stay close to him. Francis carried the rabbit into the woods and set it free. The rabbit simply followed Francis back to where he was seated and jumped onto his lap again. Finally Francis asked one of his brothers to take the rabbit deep into the forest and let it go. This time it worked—the rabbit remained content there. Such things were always happening to Francis, who saw this as a way to give praise to God.

Francis also made friends with fish. Once, he was crossing a lake with a fisherman, who caught a large fish and gave it to Francis as a gift. Francis, however, simply warned the fish not to get caught again and placed it back in the water.

Another famous story tells of a village that was under attack by a savage wolf, who had even killed some of the townspeople. Francis arranged a peaceful solution—he got the townspeople to promise to feed the wolf, if the wolf agreed to stop its violent attacks. He was able to talk with all of God's creatures, because he was sensitive to them and their needs. The incredible goodness that Francis saw in God he saw also in creatures.

Jesus and the World of Creation

Jesus of Nazareth lived his earthly life twelve centuries before St. Francis of Assisi. Long before Francis talked about the brotherhood of all creation, Jesus came to us to bring back the peace and harmony that Adam and Eve once enjoyed with the other creatures in the Garden but then, sadly, lost. Jesus surely noticed all the beauty in his world and praised his heavenly Father for it.

Jesus admired and loved the animals and other creatures, and he came into the world not only as a man but also as a brother to every creature. He praised God for caring for the birds of the air and the lilies of the field. Whether he was walking along the lakeshore, through the olive trees, or up a mountainside, Jesus always seemed at home and in harmony with the world of nature that God had created.

In his preaching, Jesus used many images from nature, telling stories of foxes, pearls, fig trees, mustard seed, weeds and wheat, and lost sheep. He understood from his knowledge of Scripture that all these things were blessed and pronounced *good* by the Creator in the beginning.

After Jesus died and rose from the dead, he appeared many times to his friends, telling them the good news that God forgives, heals, and loves all men and women, all boys and girls. Finally Jesus gathered his friends around him one last time to say goodbye. He told them he had to leave this world and return to his Father in heaven. Then he gave them an important instruction: "Go into the whole world and proclaim the gospel to every creature" (Mark 16:15). Notice that Jesus did not say *"to every human being,"* but *"to every creature."* Jesus' choice of words suggests that the gospel message is for the *whole* family of creation, not simply the human family.

The Soul of a Pet

The question "Will I see my dog (my cat, my rabbit, my gerbil, my parrot, my turtle) in heaven?" is one that is very close to our hearts. If you are reading this book, I know that you care deeply about animals. The future of our beloved pets holds deep importance for us—and it should.

Although I do not have a pet at this point in my life (unless you count Tita, a small dog who is cute as a button and often visits the Pleasant Street Friary in Cincinnati, Ohio, where I live), I have cared for and loved animals in the past. Let me tell you a story that takes me back many years.

When I was about eight years old, our family had a dog named Toppy, and my older brother, Paul, and I were supposed to take care of him. Toppy was part Beagle, and we only had him for a year or so because the poor creature got hit by a car and killed. My brother saw the accident and ran into our house, crying, telling the rest of us the terrible news. I deeply felt that loss.

For weeks and maybe months after his death, I kept expecting to see Toppy come running into our backyard where his doghouse had stood—but Toppy never showed up. That strong memory, still with me so many years later, is a clear sign of my own grief. So I understand how hard it is to lose such a loved one.

There are beloved cats living all over the world, too. Like St. Francis before us, we can care for them as brothers and sisters.

I know cats that work with hospital and nursing home volunteers, men and women who visit shut-ins, and other instances where a cat's curiosity, intelligence, and warmth brightens up the lives of those of us who need it most. I've seen people's faces light up when a cat jumps on their laps. I've seen sick people's eyes sparkle at the glimpse of a cat around the corner or in the next room. I myself was once comforted by the expression of gentle sadness and compassion that I felt from the eyes of an animal—a dog that I'll never forget named Pippy. It was as if Pippy *knew* for sure that I was sad about something.

Sometimes I think that we are able to connect with an animal in ways that we don't fully yet understand.

Cats can be quiet and peaceful companions, and so are pet rabbits, turtles, hamsters, and fish. St. Francis loved them all. So do I. I am guessing that you do, too.

All of these creatures might also remind us to pray. They all can "praise" God in their special ways, and living with them can only be a blessing.

I know some people say animals don't have souls. I agree that they don't have exactly the same kind of souls that humans have. But nobody can say that they don't have mighty hearts, a wonderful sense of play, and great abilities to give and receive love.

I feel we can make a good case for saying: yes, in some mysterious but real way, our animal, plant, and mineral companions, our "brothers" and "sisters," will be with us in paradise.

A Vision of All Creatures in Heaven

This final story is from the book of Revelation, the last book in the Bible. It's really a book of visions that the writer, St. John, saw when he was a prisoner on a Greek island called Patmos. The vision reminds us of Psalm 148, where all the creatures of the universe are praising God together.

In his vision, John saw God sitting on a glorious throne in heaven. Standing near the throne is Jesus in the form of a lamb. A big crowd of angels and people are also there before God and the Lamb. John describes the scene:

Then I heard every creature in heaven and on earth and under the earth and in the sea, everything in the universe cry out: "To the one who sits on the throne and to the Lamb be blessing and honor, glory and might, forever and ever." (Rev. 5:13 NAB)

What we see here is the whole family of creation praising God and Jesus. I believe we are all meant to walk together in peace and harmony on this earth as we journey to God.

Jesus once said that we are to have faith like children. Kids can sometimes see and understand those things that grownups, for whatever reasons, no longer seem to see or understand quite as clearly.

Many people whose pets have died have told me that they just "know" in their hearts or by some inner sense that their beloved cat or dog or parrot is in heaven. Children often have the same inner sense about their pets and other animals being in heaven.

Several first-graders at a school in my city gave these answers to my question, "Why should animals go to heaven?"

"If they didn't go to heaven, who would take care of them?"

"So they can be with their owner who loves them."

"Because it's the only place for them to go if they are good."

We may not know exactly how God will bring the whole family of creation someday to heaven. What we do know is this: our faith, along with Scripture, Christian teaching, and the life and example of St. Francis of Assisi, gives us solid hints and clues that if we live in harmony with God's plans, we will see the "whole of creation" in the world to come.

This gift of life with God in a new heaven and a new earth comes simply from God's overflowing love and goodness. God will walk side by side with all of us. "The wolf shall be the guest of the lamb" (Isa.11:6 NAB), and, hopefully, the fox will live peacefully with the rabbit, and we humans will be the happy companions and loving caregivers of our dogs and cats—and all the other creatures.

I have come to believe, "Yes, with heartfelt thanks to God's saving love for the whole family of creation, *I will see my pet in heaven!*"

Three Prayers
of Blessing

FOR ANY ANIMAL, FISH, BIRD, OR OTHER CREATURE

Gather your family and friends together for these blessings—it is good to have as much of the family of God present as possible. Insert the name of your animal companion into these prayers.

For Any of God's Creatures

Blessed are you, Lord God,
Maker of all living creatures.
On the fifth and sixth days of creation,
    you called forth fish in the sea,
    birds in the air, and animals on the land.
You inspired St. Francis to call all animals
    his brothers and sisters.
We ask you to bless this animal (these animals)
    gathered about us.
By the power of your love,
    enable him/her (them) to live according to your plan.
May we always praise you for all your beauty in creation.
Blessed are you, Lord our God, in all your creatures.
    Amen.

For One or More Sick Creatures

Heavenly Creator,
You made all things for your glory
and made us caretakers of this creature
(these creatures) under our care.
Restore to health and strength this animal
    (this pet) that you have entrusted to us.
Keep this animal (this pet)
    always under your loving protection.
Blessed are you, Lord God,
And holy is your name for ever and ever. Amen.

For an Animal That Has Died or Is About to Die

Loving God,
Our beloved pet and companion, (name),
   is on his/her final journey.
We will miss (name) dearly
   because of the joy and affection
   (name) has given to us.
Bless (name) and give him/her peace.
May your care for (name) never die.
We thank you for the gift
   that (name) has been to us.
Give us hope that in your great kindness
   you may restore (name) in your heavenly kingdom
   according to your wisdom, which goes
   beyond our human understanding. Amen.

About Paraclete Press

WHO WE ARE

Paraclete Press is a publisher of books, recordings, and DVDs on Christian spirituality. Our publishing represents a full expression of Christian belief and practice—from Catholic to Evangelical, from Protestant to Orthodox.

We are the publishing arm of the Community of Jesus, an ecumenical monastic community in the Benedictine tradition. As such, we are uniquely positioned in the marketplace without connection to a large corporation and with informal relationships to many branches and denominations of faith.

WHAT WE ARE DOING

BOOKS Paraclete publishes books that show the richness and depth of what it means to be Christian. Although Benedictine spirituality is at the heart of all that we do, we publish books that reflect the Christian experience across many cultures, time periods, and houses of worship. We publish books that nourish the vibrant life of the church and its people—books about spiritual practice, formation, history, ideas, and customs.

We have several different series, including the best-selling Paraclete Essentials and Paraclete Giants series of classic texts in contemporary English; A Voice from the Monastery—men and women monastics writing about living a spiritual life today; award-winning literary faith fiction and poetry; and the Active Prayer Series that brings creativity and liveliness to any life of prayer.

RECORDINGS From Gregorian chant to contemporary American choral works, our music recordings celebrate sacred choral music through the centuries. Paraclete distributes the recordings of the internationally acclaimed choir Gloriæ Dei Cantores, praised for their "rapt and fathomless spiritual intensity" by *American Record Guide,* and the Gloriæ Dei Cantores Schola, which specializes in the study and performance of Gregorian chant. Paraclete is also the exclusive North American distributor of the recordings of the Monastic Choir of St. Peter's Abbey in Solesmes, France, long considered to be a leading authority on Gregorian chant.

DVDs Our DVDs offer spiritual help, healing, and biblical guidance for life issues: grief and loss, marriage, forgiveness, anger management, facing death, and spiritual formation.

LEARN MORE ABOUT US AT OUR WEBSITE:
www.paracletepress.com, or call us toll-free at 1-800-451-5006.

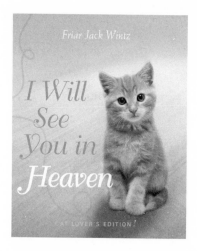